First World War
and Army of Occupation
War Diary
France, Belgium and Germany

74 (YEOMANRY) DIVISION
229 Infantry Brigade
Black Watch (Royal Highlanders)
14th (Fife and Forfar Yeo.) Battalion
16 December 1915 - 31 May 1919

WO95/3152/4

The Naval & Military Press Ltd
www.nmarchive.com
Published in association with The National Archives

Published by

The Naval & Military Press Ltd

Unit 10 Ridgewood Industrial Park,

Uckfield, East Sussex,

TN22 5QE England

Tel: +44 (0) 1825 749494

www.naval-military-press.com

www.nmarchive.com

This diary has been reprinted in facsimile from the original. Any imperfections are inevitably reproduced and the quality may fall short of modern type and cartographic standards.

© Crown Copyright
Images reproduced by permission of The National Archives, London, England, 2015.

Contents

Document type	Place/Title	Date From	Date To
Heading	WO95/3152/4 14 Battalion Black Watch (Royal Highlanders)		
Heading	74th Division 229th Infy Bde 14th Bn Roy. Hgdrs 1918 May- May 1919		
Heading	War Diary For May 1918 14th (Fife & Forfar Yeo) Bn R.H. Vol 2		
War Diary		01/05/1918	09/05/1918
War Diary	Noyelles	10/05/1918	10/05/1918
War Diary	St Firmin	11/05/1918	21/05/1918
War Diary	Humbercourt	22/05/1918	25/05/1918
War Diary	Grand Rullecourt	26/05/1918	27/06/1918
War Diary	Fontes	28/06/1918	11/07/1918
War Diary	Ham-En-Artois	12/07/1918	23/07/1918
War Diary	La Pierrierre	24/07/1918	11/08/1918
War Diary	Robecq	12/08/1918	16/08/1918
War Diary	La Miquellerie	17/08/1918	25/08/1918
War Diary	Q.3.c.8.9	26/08/1918	27/08/1918
War Diary	Molinghem	28/08/1918	29/08/1918
War Diary	La Houssoye	30/08/1918	31/08/1918
Heading	War Diary For Septr 1918 14th (F & F Yeo) Bn. R.H Vol 6		
War Diary		01/09/1918	24/09/1918
Miscellaneous	229th Brigade H.Q	02/11/1918	02/11/1918
War Diary	Bourecq	01/10/1918	02/10/1918
War Diary	Locon	03/10/1918	04/10/1918
War Diary	Herlies	05/10/1918	31/10/1918
Miscellaneous	D.A.G 3rd Echelon	30/11/1918	30/11/1918
War Diary	Baisieux	01/11/1918	02/11/1918
War Diary	Gruson	03/11/1918	08/11/1918
War Diary	Lemain	09/11/1918	09/11/1918
War Diary	Beclers	10/11/1918	10/11/1918
War Diary	Peronche	11/11/1918	11/11/1918
War Diary	Izieres	12/11/1918	16/11/1918
War Diary	Moustier	17/11/1918	15/12/1918
War Diary	Lahamaide	16/12/1915	16/12/1915
War Diary	Grammont	17/12/1918	28/02/1919
Heading	Headquarters 229 Brigade		
War Diary	Grammont	01/03/1919	31/03/1919
Miscellaneous	Headquarters 229 Brigade	30/04/1919	30/04/1919
War Diary	Grammont Belgium	01/04/1919	31/05/1919

WO95/3152/4
1t Battalion Black Watch
(Royal Highlanders)

74TH DIVISION
229TH INFY BDE

BLACK WATCH
14TH BN ROY. HGDRS
1918 MAY – ~~DEC 1918~~.
~~JAN~~ – MAY 1919.

May /18
Vol 2

713

CONFIDENTIAL

WAR DIARY FOR MAY 1918

14th (Fife & Forfar Yeo) Bn. R.H.

Army Form C. 2118.

WAR DIARY
or
INTELLIGENCE SUMMARY.
(Erase heading not required.)

Instructions regarding War Diaries and Intelligence Summaries are contained in F. S. Regs., Part II. and the Staff Manual respectively. Title pages will be prepared in manuscript.

Place	Date	Hour	Summary of Events and Information	Remarks and references to Appendices
	MAY			
	1		Voyage from ALEXANDRIA to MARSAILLES. Daily parades on board for boat and raft drill, and gas instruction.	
	2			
	3			
	4			
	5		Arrived MARSAILLES at 9 am on 4th, and disembarked at 8 pm.	
	6		Entrained at MARSAILLES at 10 pm.	
	7			
	8		Train journey continued.	
	9			
NOYELLES	10		Detrained at NOYELLES at 9.30 a.m. and marched to ST FIRMIN, where Battalion was billeted.	
ST FIRMIN	11		Battalion training, including Physical training; training with S.B. Respirators; Coy Drill and tactical schemes. Bathing and disinfection of blankets carried out at RUE.	
	12			
	13			
	14			
	15			
	16		1 Officer & 9 OR attended two days Gas Course at RUE.	
	17		2 " " " " " " " " "	
	18		1 " " Proceeded for Course of Bayonet fighting at HARDELOT PLAGE	
	19			
	20		Battalion forced through Lachrymatory Gas test.	
HUMBERCOURT	21		Battalion marched to RUE, where it entrained in two parties to HUMBERCOURT. Battalion marched to LIGNY ST FLOCHEL. On arrival at Enemy aerial enemy bombing raid in vicinity of Battalion area. No damage done.	
	22			
— do —	23		Coy and Specialist training	
	24		COL. J.B. McNAB and CAPT. D. OGILVIE proceeded on short visit to front line (NZ Division). Orders received to move following day.	

D. D. & L., London, E.C. (A8004) Wt. W1771/M.F. 31. 750,000 5/17 Sch 52 Forms/C.2118/14

Army Form C. 2118

WAR DIARY
or
INTELLIGENCE SUMMARY
(Erase heading not required.)

Place	Date	Hour	Summary of Events and Information	Remarks and references to Appendices
HUMBERCOURT	MAY 25		Battalion paraded at 9 am and marched to new billet area at GRAND RULLECOURT.	
GRAND RULLECOURT	26		Divine Service	
	27		Battalion Inspected by R.O.C. 74th Division	
	28		Musketry Practice carried out at Ranges at I.18.c.9.3. and I.14.c.4.6. (Map 51c)	
	29		Section & Platoon training	
	30		Platoon v Coy training	
	31		Battalion Tactical scheme.	

Lieut: Colonel
Commd. 14th. (Fife & Forfar Yeo) Battn.
ROYAL HIGHLANDERS

14th Bn Roy Highrs
Army Form C. 2118
JUNE 1918.

Vol 3

WAR DIARY
or
INTELLIGENCE SUMMARY
(Erase heading not required.)

Place	Date 1918 JUNE	Hour	Summary of Events and Information	Remarks and references to Appendices
GRAND RULLECOURT	1		Battn took part in Brigade Tactical Scheme	
	2		Divine Services	
	3		Physical Drill. Platoon Training Musketry at range	
	4		Tactical schemes. Training of Specialists.	
	5			
	6			
	7			
	8		Battn took part in Brigade Assault Scheme in co-operation with Tanks	
	9		Divine Service. 1 Officer & 20. O.Rs. proceeded to attend Musketry Course at 1st Army School of Musketry	
	10		Physical Drill. Company Training Musketry	
	11		Training of Specialists. Lewis Gunners. Signallers. Rifle Grenadiers etc	
	12			
	13		Gas demonstration	
	14		Tactical schemes	
	15			
	16		Divine Services	
	17		Physical Drill. Company Training. Gas Drill. Musketry at range	
	18		Specialist Training	
	19			
	20		Battn by Exercises for practice in Wood fighting	
	21			
	22			
	23		Divine Services	

Army Form C. 2118

WAR DIARY
or
INTELLIGENCE SUMMARY
(Erase heading not required.)

Place	Date 1918 JUNE	Hour	Summary of Events and Information	Remarks and references to Appendices
GRAND RULLECOURT	24			
	25		2nd Lieut H.L FRAZER (3rd R H) } Joined on " " A.R WOOD (4th R H) } posting " " J.N GRANT (6th R H) }	
	26		2nd Lieut H.ADAMSON (2nd Res R H) admitted Hospital (Sick)	
	27	5 am	Battn proceeded by route march to LIGNY ST FLOCHEL Stn, and entrained at 10.10 am	
		1.30 pm	Arrived at AIRE and immediately detrained. Marched to new billet area at FONTES. Transport travelled by road bivouacing for the night at TANGRY	
			Physical Drill, Company Training Bayonet fighting Specialist Training Practice in Wood fighting	
FONTES	28	12 noon	Transport arrived at FONTES	
	29		Lieut W.W CUMMINS is 1 o/R proceeded for duty with Divisional Reception Camp at AUCHY au BOIS	
			Company Training. Training of Specialists. Reconnaissance by officers and senior NCOs of the Sector of Defence line allotted to the Battalion	
	30		Divine Services	

Lieut: Colonel
Commd. 14th. (Fife & Forfar Yeo) Batn.
ROYAL HIGHLANDERS

714

Army Form C. 2118.

1st/1st R. of H.

July 1918

WAR DIARY
or
INTELLIGENCE SUMMARY.
(Erase heading not required.)

Instructions regarding War Diaries and Intelligence Summaries are contained in F. S. Regs., Part II. and the Staff Manual respectively. Title pages will be prepared in manuscript.

Place	Date 1918 JULY	Hour	Summary of Events and Information	Remarks and references to Appendices
FONTES	1			
	2		2nd Lt T B BROWN 4th R.H. } joined 2nd Lt F V MILLINGEN 4th R.H. } on Base	
	3		Physical Drill, Company Training, Bathing }
	4		Musketry at range. Tactical Scheme
	5		Each day a party reconnoitred the Sector & the
	6		Emergency Defence line allotted to the Battn.
	7		Inspection & fitting of Gas Respirators
	8		Divine Services	
	9		Physical Drill, Gas Training, Platoon & Coy Drill
	10		Reconnaissance of Defence line
	11		9.10. 'B' Team personnel proceeded to Dunveroal Reception Camp at WITTERNESSE
			2nd Lt H ADAMSON (R.H.) rejoined from Hospital } Battn. marched to new billet area at HAM-EN-ARTOIS.
HAM-EN-ARTOIS	12			
	13		LIEUT J S LAIRD (F&F) } proceeded to 2/K 2nd Lt A FYFE (R.H.) } for duty with R.A.F.	Platoon & Coy Training Specialist Training
	14		Divine Services	
	15			Physical Training, Company Training, Gas Drill
	16		2nd Lt R D M DANIEL (R.H.) attached 231st Bde HQ	continued with training of Specialists
	17		Capt H S SHARP (F&F) attached 74 Div HQ	Each day a party carried out reconnaissance of the
	18		'B' Team personnel rejoined from WITTERNESSE	NOC RIVER defensive line
	19		Lt S A BEARD (LANARK YEO) proceeded for duty with R.A.F.	Musketry range practice.
	20		Divine Services.	
	21			

Army Form C. 2118.

WAR DIARY
or
INTELLIGENCE SUMMARY.

(Erase heading not required.)

Instructions regarding War Diaries and Intelligence Summaries are contained in F.S. Regs., Part II. and the Staff Manual respectively. Title pages will be prepared in manuscript.

ROYAL HIGHLANDERS
Comdg. 14th. (Fife & Forfar Yeo.) Battn.
Lieut: Colonel
Manus

Place	Date 1918 JULY	Hour	Summary of Events and Information	Remarks and references to Appendices
HAM-EN-ARTOIS	22		Physical Drill, boy Training, Lectures & Bathing	
	23	2 p.m.	B Team personnel marched to billets at WITTERNESSE.	
		7 p.m.	Battn. marched to new billet area at LA PIERRIERE (Brigade Reserve)	
LA PIERRIERE	24		Boy & Specialist Training	
	25		2nd Lt G.D.M. BEARD 4th Bn R.H. joined B Team — D. McLAREN 6th - - - ex Base. Reconnaissance of Emergency Defence Line. Daily Working Party of 1 Off + 50 O/R improving Right Bn new HQ	
	26		Nightly Working Party of 4 Off + 200 O/R for work on Reserve Line	
	27		Night 24/25 1 3 O/R wounded by enemy shell fire.	
	28		Divine Services) Physical Drill, boy & Specialist Training	
	29		Daily & nightly Working Parties as above. Night 30/31st 1 man wounded	
	30		Reconnaissance of Right Sector of Bde Front.	
	31		Working Party 1 Off + 50 O/R working on new Bn HQ	
			Battn relieved the 12th (W.S.Yeo.) Bn S.L.I. in ROBECQ SECTOR of front line.	

Army Form C. 2118

14 Royal Fus 229/74

Vol 5

7/6

WAR DIARY
or
INTELLIGENCE SUMMARY
(Erase heading not required.)

Place	Date 1918 AUGT	Hour	Summary of Events and Information	Remarks and references to Appendices
	1		2nd Lieut F.J. FELL 2nd Bn RH joined from Base. Dispositions of the Battn in the line were as follows:- 1 Coy in front line posts from Q.14.c.5.9. to Q.20.b.3.9. and support line from Q.14.c.1.4. to Q.20.a.7.6. 2 Coys in Reserve line from Q.13.c.7.9. to Road in Q.19.d.3.8. 1 Coy in Right subsection of the AMUSOIRES-HAVERSKERQUE System. No gas shelling, enemy movement slight. 2 Patrols sent out, several M.G. posts located but no enemy encountered.	
	2		Situation very quiet, small individual movement observed. 1 Patrol sent out.	
	3		Situation quiet - no exceptional aerial or artillery activity. A Patrol of 1 Officer & 3 O/R encountered a party of 20 enemy. The Officer 2nd Lieut H.L.FRASER was wounded and patrol withdrew.	
	4		Situation unchanged. 3 Patrols sent out. 11 Other Ranks wounded by shell fire.	
	5		Situation normal. 6 Patrols went out to ascertain if enemy were still in position reported no signs of withdrawal.	
	6		No unusual movement. Several daylight patrols went out and found the enemy had evacuated his front line - 4 prisoners taken. The forward Coy immediately pushed forward and established themselves with 2 Platoons on a line from Q.14.d.75.60 in front of house Q.14.b.6.0. to left bank of CLARENCE RIVER at Q.14.b.15.15.	
	7		Very quiet night. Forward Coy continued to advance and by 11.30 p.m had established themselves along the line of the QUENTIN ROAD. Casualties 1 O/R KILLED 6 O/R WOUNDED	

Army Form C. 2118

WAR DIARY
or
INTELLIGENCE SUMMARY
(Erase heading not required.)

Instructions regarding War Diaries and Intelligence Summaries are contained in F. S. Regs., Part II and the Staff Manual respectively. Title Pages will be prepared in manuscript.

Place	Date 1918 AUGT.	Hour	Summary of Events and Information	Remarks and references to Appendices
	8	4.30 a.m.	An enemy party of about 30 approached one of the advanced posts but on being fired upon quickly withdrew, leaving 5 killed, the number wounded is uncertain.	
		6.30 p.m.	Enemy artillery was more active during the day and shelled with H.E. Shrapnel & Gas on the log line. The front line was again pushed forward to a line along the TURBEAUTE Stream meeting with very little opposition. Prisoners - 6. Casualties KILLED 4 Other Ranks WOUNDED 6 " "	
	9		Enemy artillery again active Bn HQ heavily bombarded with Green X N°II Gas shells. Casualties 5 Other Ranks wounded	
		9.15 p.m.		
	10	5.40 a.m. 6 a.m.	Enemy Trench mortars bombarded front line About 30 enemy attacked forward posts but were repulsed at the point of the bayonet Enemy casualties observed - 1 killed & 5 wounded	
		7 a.m.	front line again bombarded, our artillery replied and the situation became quiet. Casualties KILLED 1 Other Rank WOUNDED 6 Other Ranks	
	11		During night 10/11th Battn. was relieved by 15th Bn. the SUFFOLK Regt. Relief completed by 2 a.m. Bn. took up positions in the Reserve Line of the AMUSOIRES - HAVERSKERQUE - HAVERSKERQUE System.	

Army Form C. 2118

WAR DIARY
or
INTELLIGENCE SUMMARY
(Erase heading not required.)

Instructions regarding War Diaries and Intelligence Summaries are contained in F.S. Regs., Part II. and the Staff Manual respectively. Title Pages will be prepared in manuscript.

Place	Date 1918 AUG.	Hour	Summary of Events and Information	Remarks and references to Appendices
ROBECQ	12		Kit inspections, bathing in Canal, Physical drill.	
	13		Working Parties engaged in strengthening RESERVE LINE & CARVIN SWITCH at Q13c	
	14		in field.	
	15		Parties worked on harvesting along the ROBECQ-ST VENANT Road.	
	16		Brigade moved into Divisional Reserve, the Battn. going into Billets at LA MIQUELLERIE, taking over from 24th R.W.F. B Team rejoined from Camp at LINGHEM.	
LA MIQUELLERIE	17		Cleaning Billets, Coy. Training	
	18		Brigade Divine Service at O.28.d.3.5.80. General BIRDWOOD was present and addressed the Brigade.	
	19		Battn. was inspected by companies by the Corps Commander Sir Genl. Sir R. HAKING at HAM-EN-ARTOIS	
	20		Normal Routine.	
	21		Platoon & Specialist Training	
	22		Musketry at range.	
	23			
	24		Battn. relieved 25th R.W.F. in Brigade Reserve. Relief completed by 11.30 p.m. Bn. HQ. at Q.3.c.8.9. 2 Coys in Support at Q.4.d.2.6. 2 Coys in Support at Q.16 Central. B Team proceeded to Reception Camp at LINGHEM.	
	25	10.30 a.m	Situation very quiet. Enemy shelling cross roads in Q.3.d.4.4. to vicinity of Bn. HQ. Casualties 2 O/R. Wounded.	

WAR DIARY
or
INTELLIGENCE SUMMARY

Army Form C. 2118

Place	Date 1918 AUGT	Hour	Summary of Events and Information	Remarks and references to Appendices
Q3c89	26		The day was again quiet.	Map references 36aSE 1:20,000
	27		Battn was relieved by 2/6 DURHAM L.I. Relief completed by 2.30 a.m on 28th.	
MOLINGHEM	28	11 p.m.	Battn went into Billets at MOLINGHEM. 'B' Team rejoined. 1 Coy entrained as Brigade Advance Party.	
	29	1.30 a.m. 9 p.m.	Battn (less 1 Coy) entrained at CORBIE and marched to Billets at LA HOUSSOYE	
LA HOUSSOYE	30		Battn. remained ready to move - awaiting Orders.	
	31	2 p.m	Battn marched to Road Junction at FRAN VILLERS proceeding thence by bus to BRONFAY FARM then marched to MARICOURT where packs were dumped. Bn then proceeded to a site near the Brown Roads in B16 b 80.12 (Sheet 62c N.W.) and bivouaced for the night.	
			On 14th Chaplain R Barry Doyle (C.F) admitted Hospital	
			27 Chaplain T.L WILLIAMS (C.F) attached	
			2nd Lieut E.J STEVENSON 3rd R.H joined on posting	
			" " H. MAIR 2nd R.H " "	
			30 " " W.O GILCHRIST 7 R.H " "	

A.D.Ogilvie Major
Commd. 14th (F&F) Bn
ROYAL HIGHLANDERS

CONFIDENTIAL.

WAR DIARY FOR SEPTR 1918.

14TH (F.&F.Yeo) Bn. R.H.

Army Form C. 2118

4th Bn. Royal Highlanders

WAR DIARY
or
INTELLIGENCE SUMMARY
(Erase heading not required.)

Place	Date 1918 Sept	Hour	Summary of Events and Information	Remarks and references to Appendices
	1		Battalion moved from B.16.d.80.12 (Sheet 62.c.N.W.) at 7.30 pm and bivouaced to trench at C.15.d.2.6 where 6th Batt H.A.C. were established. Relieved the London Regt. during the night. Coys. occupying assembly trenches preparatory to the attack the following morning.	
	2		After preliminary bombardment, Brigade moved forward to the attack. Immediately the Village of MOISLAINS (Sheet 62.c.N.W. 1/20,000, C.12.v.18) was taken. The Batt. moved to left to take its objective MONASTIR TRENCH, thence along Canal to v along OPERA TRENCH. The 2nd objective being oblique line running through D.2.c., D.8. and D.14.b. The first objective was gained and Batt was closely in to 2nd objective when heavy M.G. fire was opened on left flank from MOISLAINS. Batt. of London Regt. on left withdrew, leaving flank exposed to M.G. fire and Batt. was compelled to withdraw. Village of MOISLAINS was inadequately mopped up & M.G. fire was opened from south of village. Battalion assembled in trench in C.22.d. and SCUTARI TRENCH C.28.a. Casualties:- Killed 3 officers 36 O.Rs. Wounded 11 " 154 "	
	3		Batt. assembled in ANBORA TRENCH, C.16, where it was formed into 2 Composite Coys. under Lieut. J.W. ARNOTT. Patrols pushed out during the day and posts were established at dusk on SLAG HEAP C.24.a.9.2 and in trench C.17.d.8.7. Night was quiet.	
	4		Composite Coy. gradually moved forward and took up new line in trench along Canal Bank in C.18.c.d. At dusk, the Batt. was relieved by 19th Batt. London Regt. and when relief was complete Batt. moved to N edge of wood in C.25.a.b. Organisation into Batt. and burial of our dead.	
	5			
	6		Battalion marched to AIZECOURT and bivouaced for the night at J.7.c.40.40	

Army Form C. 2118

WAR DIARY
or
INTELLIGENCE SUMMARY
(Erase heading not required.)

Instructions regarding War Diaries and Intelligence Summaries are contained in F.S. Regs., Part II. and the Staff Manual respectively. Title Pages will be prepared in manuscript.

Place	Date 1918	Hour	Summary of Events and Information	Remarks and references to Appendices
	Sept 4		Batt. left AIZECOURT at 3:30 p.m. and marched to LONGAVESNES, E.25.	
	8		Batt. relieved 25th Batt. Welch Regt. in F.13.c.7.d. and F.19.c.v.d. During the night enemy shelled valley about E.23.8 with approx. 50 rounds Blue X Gas Shells	
	9		Dispositions of Batt. in the line were as follows:- S/Coy from F.13.c.5.10 to road in F.19.8 "" F.19.6. to F.19.c.10.5. 12 Coys " F.19.6. to F.19.c.10.5. Numerous patrols pushed out and all reported trench running E&W through F.13.d and F.14.c&d to be occupied, so also trench running N&S through F.20.L&d. Enemy sniped at and fired upon by M.G. from BOULEAUX WOODS. F.25.c and from ridge along road in F.20.a
Two patrols received to make good ridge in & about F.26.a. RONSSOY - BASSEE BOULOGNE thence N.W. to F.9.c. As soon as patrols approached positions, they were met with heavy fire and operation was found impracticable	
	10		In co-operation with 58th Division on left & 16th Devon Regt. on right, the Batt. (less 1 Coy in support) moved forward after a preliminary bombardment to occupy objectives - Trench running E&W through F.13.d & F.14.c&d, and trench running N&S through F.20.L&d. On reaching these trenches they were found heavily manned and our Coys were heavily fired upon by M.G. fire. Batt. was severely enfiladed from ridge on left and only course open was to withdraw to their positions.
Casualties:- Killed   -   4 O.R.s
Wounded 2 Officers 23 "
Missing 26 "	

WAR DIARY
or
INTELLIGENCE SUMMARY

(Erase heading not required.)

Army Form C. 2118

Instructions regarding War Diaries and Intelligence Summaries are contained in F.S. Regs., Part II. and the Staff Manual respectively. Title Pages will be prepared in manuscript.

Place	Date 1918 April	Hour	Summary of Events and Information	Remarks and references to Appendices
	11.		Battalion was relieved at night by 10th East Kent Regt. and on completion of relief Batt marched back to trenches at LONGAVESNES, E.26.a.d. Draft of 11 Officers and 4 other ranks joined from Base.	
	12.		Battalion moved to vicinity of TEMPLEUX-LA-FOSSE where Coys were established along trench beside ARCHE WOOD running through D.29 & S.8. to D.23.c.y.5 to edge of CHAPEL WOOD.	
	13.		Day spent in looking and cleaning up. Draft of 60 other ranks joined from Base.	
	14.		Training under Coy arrangements	
	15.		Divine Service.	
	16.		Platoon & Lewis Gun training. Salvage parties cleared ground as follows:- Squares D.14; D.18 and D.23.	
	17.		Battalion (less Coy) marched to training area in FAUSTINE QUARRY in K.5.d. Draft of 1 Officer and 23 other ranks joined from Base.	
	18.		1 Coy attached to 10th S.L.I. were in support to 830th Bde. In the morning, after a Preliminary Bombardment Coy advanced to sunken road near PIMPLE POST in F.25.c. They then advanced towards Red Line from BENJAMIN POST to HUSSAR POST in F.23.d. to F.29.d. but while they were held up by M.G. fire from RIFLEMAN POST in F.29.b., but our Artillery dealt with this and RIFLEMAN POST was rendered and reoccupated. During this operation our Coy took a number of prisoners and machine guns Casualties:- Killed – 4 other ranks. Wounded 1 Officer 24 do.	

WAR DIARY
or
INTELLIGENCE SUMMARY
(Erase heading not required.)

Army Form C. 2118

Place	Date 1918 Sept.	Hour	Summary of Events and Information	Remarks and references to Appendices
	19.		Search party went out to F.20.c.d to search for missing men reported on 10th inst. First bodies were found and identified and buried. Draft of 41 other ranks joined from the Base. Coy attached to 12th S.L.I. was relieved by Sussex Regt. and marched to K.6.d.23 where they took over bivouac area	
	20.		Salvage Parties cleared the following areas: L.1; L.2; L.3 and K.6 Battalion took over line from 7th Suffolk Regt. from F.28.b.4.5 to F.28.c.3.0.	
	21.		Patrols sent out from each Coy to reconnoitre r/s to line from F.23.d.8.3 to F.29.d.4.8. Enemy shelled our lines repeatedly with 5.9 H.E. and Green Cross shells.	
	22.		Patrol sent out from right Coy to reconnoitre r/s to line in F.29.d.4.8. Battalion moved forward and took over line from BENJAMIN POST F.23.d.8.3 to FIRE PIT TRENCH F.30.c.4.4. with 1 Coy in support at ARTAXERE'S POST F.29.c.3.4. Enemy shelled front line at intervals all day with 5.9 H.E. & Gas shells 5 o/r's Casualties:- Killed 1 Officer 15 " Wounded	
	23.		Patrols sent out during night of 22nd/23rd to reconnoitre ground in front. No enemy were encountered & patrols returned safely. Consolidated two O.P.s at F.23.8.3 and at HUSSAR POST F.29.d.5.9. Enemy shelled front line and support with 5.9 H.E. and Green Cross Gas shells. Casualties:- Killed 1 O.R. Wounded 6 "	

Army Form C. 2118

WAR DIARY
or
INTELLIGENCE SUMMARY
(Erase heading not required.)

Instructions regarding War Diaries and Intelligence Summaries are contained in F. S. Regs., Part II. and the Staff Manual respectively. Title Pages will be prepared in manuscript.

Place	Date 1918 Sept.	Hour	Summary of Events and Information	Remarks and references to Appendices
	24		Two unsuccessful attempts were made to patrol TROLLOPE TRENCH in A25.c.5.0. Enemy put down M.G. barrage in front of our lines and rendered movement forward impossible. Enemy shelled front line at intervals with 5.9 H.E. and Yellow Cross Gas shells. Casualties:- Killed - Wounded 1 Officer 6 "	
	25		Draft of 1 Officer and 26 O/Rs joined from Base. Battalion relieved on night of 24/25th by 106th American Battalion, and on completion of relief Batt. marched to Tincourt area at FAUSTINE QUARRY in Square K.5.d.	
	26		Batt. left FAUSTINE QUARRY at 8 am and marched to TINCOURT where they entrained for VILLIERS BRETTONEUX. Marched from there to CORBIE and took over billets there.	
	27		Day spent in cleaning equipment and clothing. Training under Coy. arrangements.	
	28		Battalion left CORBIE and marched to MERICOURT L'ABBÉ and entrained for BERGUETTE at 3 pm.	
	29		Battalion detrained at BERGUETTE and marched to BOURECQ and took over billets there.	
	30		Training under Coy. arrangements. Battalion took over line of baths at HAM-EN-ARTOIS.	

WAR DIARY or INTELLIGENCE SUMMARY

Army Form C. 2118

(Erase heading not required.)

Place	Date 1918	Hour	Summary of Events and Information	Remarks and references to Appendices
	Sept 2		Movement of Officers for month:	
			Capt J.C. Martin — Fife & Forfar Yeo	} Killed in Action
			2/Lt R.W. Stewart — do — Yeo	
			2/Lt C.E. Darney — Y/R Black Watch	
			2/Lt G. Younger — Fife & Forfar Yeo	
			2/Lt J. Duncan — do —	
			2/Lt R.C. Drysdale — do —	
			2/Lt R.A. Clydesdale — do —	
			Capt J.B. McNab — 5th Black Watch	} Wounded admitted Hospital
			2/Lt S.C. Ewing — 4th do.	
			2/Lt T. Knott — 6th do.	
			2/Lt J.W. Dowes — 6th do.	
			2/Lt L. van Millingen — 6/2 do.	
			2/Lt J.W. Granger — 4th Gordon Hdrs	
			2/Lt J.A. Jackie — 4th do.	— do —
			2/Lt J. McLean — 14th R.H.	
			2/Lt W. Cruickshank — 6th Seaforths	
	10		Supt n/f J. Steele — 6th Black Watch	} James on Posting
			2/Lt J. Paterton — 3rd do	
			" J. Elgar — 3rd do	
			" G.C. Brown — 6th do	
			" P. McD. Rameo — 3rd do	
			" W. Davidson — 3rd do	
			" W.A. McMahon — 3rd do	
			" J.K. Cumming — 3rd do	
			" H.O. Bryant — 11th do	
	11		2/Lt G.C. Drummond — 3rd do	
			" J.J. Marbrener — 3rd do	

WAR DIARY
or
INTELLIGENCE SUMMARY

Army Form C. 2118

Place	Date	Hour	Summary of Events and Information	Remarks and references to Appendices
	1918 Sept		Movement of Officers (contd):-	
	14		Lieut Col J.M. McKenzie D.S.O. of Royal Scots — Joined on posting	
	18		2/Lieut T.C. Stuart 1/4 Black Watch — Wounded & admitted Hospital	
	22		—"— D. McInnes 3rd do — do	
	—"—		—"— L.J. Bell 2nd do — do	
	24		Lieut J.B. Prentice Fife & Forfar Yeo. Joined on posting	

J.M. McKenzie
Lieut: Colonel
Commd. 14th (Fife & Forfar Yeo) Battn.
ROYAL HIGHLANDERS

229th Brigade H.Q.

Herewith please copy of War
Diary for month of October
1917.

John MacKenzie
Lieut. Colonel
Comdg. 7th (F[ife] & Forfar Yeo.) Bn.
ROYAL HIGHLANDERS

2-11-18

Army Form C. 2118

WAR DIARY
or
INTELLIGENCE SUMMARY
(Erase heading not required.)

Instructions regarding War Diaries and Intelligence Summaries are contained in F.S. Regs., Part II. and the Staff Manual respectively. Title Pages will be prepared in manuscript.

1/4 R/us Regiment

Vol 7

Place	Date 1918 Oct	Hour	Summary of Events and Information	Remarks and references to Appendices
BOURECQ	1		Training under Coy arrangements. 1 Coy had use of the baths at HAM EN ARTOIS.	
	2		Battalion left BOURECQ and marched to BURBURE and entrained on light railway for LOCON. Sketch & Wire	
LOCON	3		Training under Coy arrangements. Battalion left LOCON at 1900 and marched to bivouac area in M.35 W and M.35.	
	4		Battalion left above area and marched to HERLIES in T.14.d	
HERLIES	5		Specialist training under Coy arrangements	
	6		Coys employed in their respective areas digging trenches and strongpoints round their sub	
	7		Training under Coy arrangements. Coy Commanders reconnoitred Battle positions in T.11, T.14, T.19 and T.18. 2 Left Coy officers and 60 Bayonets from the Base	
	8		Training under Coy arrangements, special attention being paid to L.G. training Lecture by M.O. to various Coys on Trench Feet	
	9		Training under Coy arrangements, 4 officers joined from Base. Coy Commanders reconnoitred new area to be occupied	
	10		Battalion left HERLIES and marched to new area in O.26 d and O.32 B.	
	11		Coys engaged in digging a outpost outpost line and putting the Wide Ditch near LA FLEUR en Wide Ditch men to bridge it Reconnaissance of forward positions carried out.	

Nov 12 on the line 7B

WAR DIARY or INTELLIGENCE SUMMARY

Army Form C. 2118

Place	Date 1918 Oct	Hour	Summary of Events and Information	Remarks and references to Appendices
	12		Work continued on Outpost Line	
	13			
	14		Work continued on Outpost Line. During the night the Battalion moved into the line and relieved 12th Bn. S.L.I. The right Coy. the line and one in outpost. Batt. HQrs remained at same place. O.36.d.3.4.	
	15		Patrol finding Railway embankment free of enemy, Coys moved forward and occupied embankment O.23.a,c and O.29.b&d (Sheet 36.S.W) Patrols found and ahead full 6 strongpoints left were held up by M.G. in LES HABOURDIN FARM, O.18.c. Line was established running through O.24.a,c and O.30.a,c. During the day others were received for advance but as first objective had not been reached, line remained stationary during night 15th/16th. Casualties:- Wounded 1 Officer + 3 O.Rs.	
	16		In the morning line was again advanced, but it was found impossible to reach 1st objective owing to heavy hostile M.G. fire from FROMEZ FARM, P.26.c and Nth P.25.a.d. In the evening 16th Devon Batt took over East half of our line from our Boundary at P.13.c.10.8 to road P.19.d.4.5. Thence running South to O.30.c.6.0.6.0. Patrols sent out at dawn reported all clear up to 1st objective on target immediately. Line moved forward and occupied objective viz from P.20.b.95.50 to Enter Rte. boundary at P.27.d.2.0 with 1 Coy in outpost and 1 Coy in reserve. Patrols found on through HAUBOURDIN and occupying new objective running over HAUTE DEULE CANAL; 2nd objective road running from Southern Batt Boundary at P.10.a.6.3; 3rd objective line Q.25.6.50 westward through Q.25.a, P.25.b, P.24.d.c.: P.28.a.y.0 through P.28.a, P.22.c.a, P.16.c.a to Northern Batt Boundary at ENNEQUIN thence through P.23.b, P.17.d.v.b. and Pn E.	
	17			

WAR DIARY
or
INTELLIGENCE SUMMARY

(Erase heading not required.)

Army Form C. 2118

Instructions regarding War Diaries and Intelligence Summaries are contained in F. S. Regs., Part II. and the Staff Manual respectively. Title Pages will be prepared in manuscript.

Place	Date 1918 Oct	Hour	Summary of Events and Information	Remarks and references to Appendices
	17 (contd)		When 3rd objective was reached 16th Devons moved through our Batt. to continue advance to line of Railway Q.14.B.80. through Q.18.C, Q.24 and to Q.30.C.4.O. and Battalion remained in outpost. Advanced guard was formed and Batt. moved in Column of route into transport to PETIT RONSHIN, where they billeted for the night.	
	18		Battalion moved off at 0930 and marched to ASCQ, remaining in support to 16th Devons. 2 Coys and HWQ were billeted in village, 2 the two Coys forming a outpost outpost line in front of village New R.H.EWART. 97.63.70.) and 2/Lieut D.McLINNES, 3/5 B.W. reported having died of wounds.	
	19.		Battalion lay in ASCQ all day. Orders for further advance were issued 1st objective N.55 central, N.19 to N.13 central; 2nd objective N.28 central, N.22 to N.16 central. 12th S.L.I. formed advanced guard, this 6 Batt. to move 1000 yds in rear in support. Batt. marched from ASCQ at 1800 and billeted for night at BAISIEUX, two Coys formed outpost outpost line approx 500 yds in front of village.	
	20		Battalion marched from BAISIEUX at 0815, but owing to 12.K.S.L.I. being held up outside MARQUAIN, had to remain on road during the day in the vicinity of Cross Roads N.21.d. 1 Coy sent forward to MARQUAIN to be at the disposal of 12th S.L.I.	
	21.		Battalion moved forward to MARQUAIN where they billeted for the night, two Coys forming an outpost line. Casualties:- Killed 1 O.R.; Wounded 3 O.Rs	

WAR DIARY
or
INTELLIGENCE SUMMARY
(Erase heading not required.)

Army Form C. 2118

Places	Date	Hour	Summary of Events and Information	Remarks and references to Appendices
	1918 Oct			
	22		Battalion relieved 10th R.S.L.I. in the line with three Coys in the line and 1 Coy in support in ORCQ. Much hostile M.G. fire during the night. Patrols sent out, but were unable to advance far owing to M.G. fire.	
	23		Day fairly quiet. At 4.30 p.m. Brigade Orders of dinner on right of line were received to advance our right flank to sunken road running N. & S. through O.24.c. Attack was made by "C" Coy with 1 Platoon advancing to Windmill and 1 Platoon to Grou Garde. Both Platoons were held up within 100 yards of objective by intense M.G. fire and T.M's. Artillery barrage was also heavy and Coy was compelled to withdraw to original line. Casualties:- Killed 1 Officer 8 O.Rs Wounded 1 " 22 " N.Y.K.O.O. 1 " 5 "	
	24.		Patrols were out during the night and found sunken road strongly held. Day very quiet. In the evening Batt. was relieved by 10./K.G./O. Yeu Yeo Bn Left Buffs. On completion of relief Battalion marched back to billets in THISIEUX.	
	25.		Day spent in cleaning up and resting. 2 Officers joined from Base.	
	26.		Specialist training made. Coy arrangements Divine Service.	
	27.		Training under Coy arrangements	
	28.		Coy training; musketry; map reading and writing of reports by Junior Officers; and practice of night patrolling.	
	29.		Battalion had the use of the Baths	

WAR DIARY or INTELLIGENCE SUMMARY

Army Form C. 2118

Command. 14th (Fife & Forfar Yeo.) Battn. ROYAL HIGHLANDERS
Lieut: Colonel

Place	Date	Hour	Summary of Events and Information	Remarks and references to Appendices
	1918 Oct 30.		Platoon & Section training etc; map reading and writing of reports for all Sergts.	
	31.		Platoon training etc. Battalion had the use of the range.	
			Movement of Officers for the month:-	
			Lieut. D.J. Edmonds 10th R.B.W. Joined from Base - 4/10/18.	
			" R.W. Ewart 9th "	
			" R.W. Ross 2nd "	
			" J. Taylor-Bowen 3rd "	
			" A.S. MacKenzie 5th "	
			2/Lieut. L. Gilbert M.M. 3rd "	
			2/Lieut. L. Gilbert M.M. 3rd R.H. To U.K. for duty with M.G. Corps - 14/10/18	
			" E.J. Alexander. 3rd R.H. Wounded admitted Hospital - 15/10/18	
			Lieut. R.W. Ewart 9th R.H. ---- do ---- 16/10/18	
			2/Lieut. R.O. Wood D.C.M. M.M. 4th R.H.	
			Lieut. W.C. Smith M.C. L/L. Yeo. To U.K. to attend Instructors Course - 23/10/18	
			2/Lieut. J.K. Gumming 3rd R.H. Killed in Action - 23/10/18	
			" R. Ralston " Wounded admitted Hospital - 23/10/18	
			Capt. T.C.S. Moir 4th Gordon Hrs Joined from Base - 25/10/18	
			2/Lt. G. Anderson 3rd R.H.	
			" Brig. Tucker 10th R.H. ---- do ---- 24/10/18	
			Lieut. L.S.R. Morgan	

D.A.G.
3rd Echelon.

5

No. D/8
3/11/18

Herewith original copy of A.F.C.2118 (War Diary) of the 14th Bn. The Royal Highlanders for the month of NOVEMBER 1918.

J.M. Mackenzie Lt. Colonel
ROYAL HIGHLANDERS

14th R. Highld Army Form C. 2118
227 74
Vol 8

WAR DIARY
or
INTELLIGENCE SUMMARY
(Erase heading not required.)

Instructions regarding War Diaries and Intelligence Summaries are contained in F.S. Regs., Part II. and the Staff Manual respectively. Title Pages will be prepared in manuscript.

Place	Date 1916 Nov	Hour	Summary of Events and Information	Remarks and references to Appendices
BRAISIEUX	1		Training as usual. B and C Coys had the use of rifle range. Demonstration of no 27 Smoke Rifle Grenade (by ord. of 1st Coy. Specialists under inspection officer for training. Casualties: 1 Officer / Capt & Adjt R. H. Coltheart) and 3 Ranks wounded. 10 R wounded remained on duty.	misnet
	2		Training as usual. Specialists under respective officers. A and D Coys had the use of rifle range. Casualty: 1 Off. (Capt & Adjt R. H. Coltheart) was Adjt of 14 months.	
GRUSON	3		Batt. Parade for Divine Service at 10.30. Arrived at 14.00 to new billeting area at GRUSON.	
	4		Training of Platoons under Platoon Officers. Specialist training under respective officers. Remained training in afternoon.	
	5		Coys cleaned equipment in billets and also rifles, owing to wet weather. On two Platoon returns to billets. Batt. Intelligence Officer attended meeting at Brigade H.Q. at CAMPHIN of Intelligence Officers of the Bd to discuss matters relating to training and to their establishment strength.	
	6		Platoons did 1/2 hr training under Platoon Officers in morning. Remainder of morning under Company arrangements. Surprise inspection by G.O.C. Bn. at 14.00 cancelled today in bad weather.	
	7		Batt. Paraded at 9.00 for inspection by G.O.C. Div. in football ground at GRUSON. Coys of newest training in afternoon. Marching order revised at 18.00 for Batt. to move tomorrow totals on from Bn of Bde of 55th Division on night 8/9.	719
	8		Relief 1 Bd of 53rd Brit cancelled. 1/2 hr Platoon training. Remainder of morning at disposal of Coy Commanders. Bn of Highlanders remained in billets. Billeting party proceeded to reconnoitre new billets at LEMAIN. As Bn did not move this afternoon these not cancelled later.	

Army Form C. 2118

WAR DIARY
or
INTELLIGENCE SUMMARY
(Erase heading not required.)

Instructions regarding War Diaries and Intelligence Summaries are contained in F. S. Regs., Part II. and the Staff Manual respectively. Title Pages will be prepared in manuscript.

Place	Date 1918	Hour	Summary of Events and Information	Remarks and references to Appendices
LEMAIN	9		Germans evacuated TOURNAI. Battalion moved at 1000 to LEMAIN and HAUDION. A and C Coys at the latter place in billets. Bgre B and D Coys at LEMAIN.	
BECLERS	10		Batt moved on at 0900, and marched to new billet area at BECLERS where it remained for the night.	
PERONCHE	11		" " " " " PERONCHE " " "	
			Orders received en route for Bde to stop where they happened to be as Armistice had been signed and hostilities would cease at 1100. This order subsequently cancelled and Batt marched on arriving 17.30.	
JZIERES	12		Batt moved on again to JZIERES. 229th Bde relieved 23rd Bde. Decr Arm Batt in billets. Prov'lg picquets. Royal Highlanders in reserve.	
	13		Batt paraded for church for road cleaning in the Battr billet area. Recreational training in afternoon.	
	14		A and C Coys worked on roads. B and D Coys did 1 hr training under Platoon Commanders - remainder of morning at the disposal of Coy. Pt Officers for cleaning billets etc. M.O. lectured to foremen to all Coys on character. General Recreational training in afternoon. Outpost groups furnished by Bde to Armd Batt relieving Arm Bucks. Farm Batt.	
	15		1 hr Platoon training under Platoon Officers - remainder afternoon under Coys arrangements. Recreational training in afternoon	
	16		B and C Coys on suspects in morning by Commanding Officer. A and D Coys did 1 hr Platoon training under Platoon Officers - remainder of forenoon at disposal of Coy Commanders. Recreational training in afternoon.	
	17		Batt moved to new billet area at MOUSTIER at 0830. Billeting party proceeded in advance.	
MOUSTIER	18		A and C Coys went out for work on roads near LEUZE at 0700. B and D Coys remained in billets owing to (a) market.	
	19		Coys at disposal of Coy Commanders in forenoon. Recreational training in afternoon. All available NCO's parade at 1400 for Communication Drill by M.D. under the R.S.M. All work on roads cancelled for the Batt. 74.5 Div. was transferred to SECOND ARMY	

1875 W. W593/826 1,000,000 4/15 J.B.C. & A. A.D.S.S./Forms/C. 2118.

Army Form C. 2118

WAR DIARY
or
INTELLIGENCE SUMMARY
(Erase heading not required.)

Instructions regarding War Diaries and Intelligence Summaries are contained in F. S. Regs., Part II. and the Staff Manual respectively. Title Pages will be prepared in manuscript.

Place	Date Nov 1918	Hour	Summary of Events and Information	Remarks and references to Appendices
MONSTIER	20		All Coys, HQrs & Transport went to Divisional Baths during today. D Coy escorted by Commanding Officer in morning. Recreational training in afternoon. Meeting of Educational Officers 3rd Bde Inspn DD Ogilvie Bath representative attended.	
	21		The whole Battalion employed on work on roads near LEUZE.	
	22		A Coy inspected by Commanding Officer. B, C and D Coys went for route march. Recreational training in afternoon. Para typhoid re-inoculation carried out in afternoon by M.O.	
	23		Batt" under Bde arrangements for 1st line. Afterwards Batt" drill under C.O. Recreational training in afternoon. III Corps (including 74th Bn) retransferred into Fifth Army.	
	24		Divine Service at 10.30.	
	25		Batt" went for Route March. Recreational training in afternoon.	
	26		Coys did three skeleton Batt" drill in morning. Blankets also fumigated in Foden Lorry disinfector. Batt" medically inspected by M.O. Recreational training.	
	27		Ceremonial Drill under C.O. Lieut Col T. YOUNGER - late Comdg 10th Battn awarded the D.S.O. Recreation in afternoon.	
	28		Route March at 0900.	
	29		All Coys sent in morning cleaning roads in billet area. Recreational training in afternoon. Officers training urge repelling attacks.	
	30		Musketry Practice on improvised ranges in morning. Football match in afternoon.	

Army Form C. 2118

WAR DIARY
or
INTELLIGENCE SUMMARY
(Erase heading not required.)

Places	Date	Hour	Summary of Events and Information	Remarks and references to Appendices
MOUSTIER	1918 Nov		Movements of Officers during the month of NOVEMBER:—	
	2		Capt R.H. COLTHART proceeded on leave	
	3		" J.D. BEVERIDGE Admitted to Hospital	
	15		2nd Lieut N.B. CLAYTON } Joined from Base	
			" R. THOMSON }	
			" J. BURNSIDE }	
	9		" W.R. DICKSON Transferred 6th.T.M.B.	
	19		" G.S. WALKER } Joined from Base	
			" H.O. FRASER }	
	21		" E.J. STEVENSON " " "	
	24		" H.L. FRASER } " " "	
			" J.W.M. GOURLAY }	
	29		Major D.D. OGILVIE To ENGLAND on Educational Course	

Jn. Mackenzie
Lieut: Colonel
Commd. 14th. (Fife & Forfar Yeo.) Bt'n.
ROYAL HIGHLANDERS

Dec/18.
Army Form C. 2118.
14th Bn Roy Irish

WAR DIARY
or
INTELLIGENCE SUMMARY.

Place	Date	Hour	Summary of Events and Information	Remarks and references to Appendices
MOUSTIER	1		Divine Service at 10.30. Rest in day.	
	2		Battalion had the use of Divisional Baths at FRASNES during day. Recreational training in afternoon.	
	3		2 Coys went on Route March - 2 Coys practised Ceremonial drill in preparation for King's visit. Recreational training in afternoon. N.C.O.s paraded under R.S.M. in afternoon.	
	4		Coys cleaning equipment for proposed inspection by King George on Saturday next. Composite Coys of men selected to form Guard of Honour carried out practice Ceremonial. Recreational training in afternoon.	F.20
	5		Rehearsal by Guard of Honour for King's Visit. 80 O.R. per Coy selected and 3 officers per Coy. Rest of morning cleaning equipment and practice Ceremonial Drill. Afternoon - Recreational training.	

Army Form C. 2118.

WAR DIARY
or
INTELLIGENCE SUMMARY.
(Erase heading not required.)

Instructions regarding War Diaries and Intelligence Summaries are contained in F. S. Regs., Part II. and the Staff Manual respectively. Title pages will be prepared in manuscript.

Place	Date	Hour	Summary of Events and Information	Remarks and references to Appendices
MOUSTIER	6	11.00	Practice Guard of the Remainder of Battalion doing Ceremonial etc. Recreational Training in Afternoon.	Ceremonial Guard of Honour Cancelled.
	7		Battalion paraded at 06.45 and marched to point on LEUZE – TOURNAI Road near BARRY (Q.3.n.d.)(Sheet 37) for visit of King George V. King arrived at 12.35 and walked along the Road – Informal inspection was allowed to break ranks. Batt. then marched home arriving back about 15.45.	
	8		Divine Service at 10.15 – Battalion Paraded.	
	9		Training under Company Arrangements also Educational training – Recreational in afternoon.	
	10			
	11			
	12		Wet day. Battalion had the usual Divisional Battle of FRASNES throughout the day. – Educational training.	

Army Form C. 2118.

WAR DIARY
or
INTELLIGENCE SUMMARY.
(Erase heading not required.)

Place	Date 1915 December	Hour	Summary of Events and Information	Remarks and references to Appendices
MOUSTIER	13		Wet day. Part Battalion went for Route march, but returned early owing to inclement weather. Remainder of Battalion was on "Educational Training" - Educational Pictures shewing in Afternoon.	
	14		Kings Birthday Anniversary. Battalion Educational Training. Afternoon - Half Holiday.	
	15		Battalion moved to new Billeting Area, and arrived at LAHAMAIDE about 15.30. 2/Lt S.S. Hooson went ahead to prepare billet for the night. Left MOUSTIER at 11.30. Billeting Party under	
LAHAMAIDE	16		The Battalion left LAHAMAIDE at 0900 and halted from 11.50 to 13.00 for mid-day meal and then proceeded to GRAMMONT arriving about 15.30	
GRAMMONT	17		Battalion cleaning up, arranging billets and Battalion Recreational Training in Afternoon.	

Army Form C. 2118.

WAR DIARY
or
INTELLIGENCE SUMMARY.

(Erase heading not required.)

Instructions regarding War Diaries and Intelligence Summaries are contained in F. S. Regs., Part II. and the Staff Manual respectively. Title pages will be prepared in manuscript.

Place	Date	Hour	Summary of Events and Information	Remarks and references to Appendices
GRAMMONT	1918 Decem. 18		Educational & Recreational Training	
	19			
	20		Rest moved in morning. Educational training in Afternoon	
	21		Divine Service — Battalion paraded at 10.0 hours. Recreational training in Afternoon	
	22			
	23		Rest moved in morning. Educational training and Games in Afternoon	
	24	08.30 10.15	Military training. Coys met Coy Arrangements. Recreational training in Afternoon	
	25		Christmas Day — Whole Holiday. Football matches in Afternoon	
	26		Whole Holiday — Coys played Football during afternoon	
	27		Battalion had the use of the Baths during the day. Recreational training in Afternoon and Evening.	

Army Form C. 2118

WAR DIARY
or
INTELLIGENCE SUMMARY
(Erase heading not required.)

Instructions regarding War Diaries and Intelligence Summaries are contained in F. S. Regs., Part II. and the Staff Manual respectively. Title Pages will be prepared in manuscript.

Place	Date 1918 December	Hour	Summary of Events and Information	Remarks and references to Appendices
GRAMMONT	28		Educational training in morning, Indoor Recreational training in Afternoon.	
	29		Sunday. Voluntary Service for Presbyterians in Afternoon.	
	30		Educational training in morning. Football match and Recreational training in Afternoon.	
	31		Bn's. moved in morning. Coy. inter-league football matches in Afternoon.	

Movement of Officers during month

Lieut R.A. Longhill (F&F Yeo) Joined on Posting 12-12-18.
Lieut J.R. Prentice (F&F Yeo) Proceeded to UK for demobilyzation 27-12-18.

McOnucher Capt
for Lieut-Colonel
Commd. 14th (F'fe & Forfar Yeo) Battn.
ROYAL HIGHLANDERS

14 R.F.
F.H.

98 10

WAR DIARY
or
INTELLIGENCE SUMMARY.
(Erase heading not required.)

Army Form C. 2118.

Instructions regarding War Diaries and Intelligence Summaries are contained in F. S. Regs., Part II. and the Staff Manual respectively. Title pages will be prepared in manuscript.

Place	Date	Hour	Summary of Events and Information	Remarks and references to Appendices
GRAMMONT	1918 January 1		Whole Holiday	
	2	08.30 / 12.00	Military and Educational Training	
	3		Afternoon – Recreational Training	
	4		Route March. Afternoon – Holiday	
	5	11.00	Church Parade in Recreation Hall	
	6	08.30 / 12.00	Military and Educational Training. Afternoon – Batt. football match against 16th Devons	
	7	09.00 / 12.00	Presentations of Ribbons in Market Place by G.O.C. Afternoon – Recreational Training	
	8	08.30 / 12.00	Military and Educational Training – Afternoon – Football matches	
	9	07.30 / 12.00	Military and Educational Training. Afternoon – Recreational Training. Batt. Pt. Course started in Recreation Hall.	
	10	09.00 / 12.00	Route March. Afternoon – Coy. Inter League football Matches	
	11		Bath had the use of The Baths. Two Coys on Route march – Educational training – Lecture on Demobilisation – Football match. Senr Level of Div Cat. 14th RH Versus 8th K.S.L.I.	7

WAR DIARY
or
INTELLIGENCE SUMMARY.
(Erase heading not required.)

Army Form C. 2118.

Place	Date	Hour	Summary of Events and Information	Remarks and references to Appendices
GRAMMONT	1918 January 12	09.30	Church Parade in Recreation Hall	
	13	08.30 / 12.15	Military and Educational Training. Afternoon. Recreational Training	
	14	09.00 / 12.15	Route March. Afternoon. Recreational Training. Coy Interleague Football	
	15	08.30 / 12.15	Military Educational Training. Afternoon. Recreational Training	
	16	09.00 / 12.00	Route March. Afternoon. Recreational Training	
	17		Military and Educational Training. Afternoon. Recreational Training	
	18		Giving Service in Recreation Hall	
	19	08.30 / 12.15	Military and Educational Training. Afternoon Football match	
	20		Semi final of Div Cup Replayed - 14th R.H.Y. 10½ K.S.L.I.	
	21	09.00 / 12.15	Route March. Afternoon. Recreational Training. Coy Interleague Football	
	22	08.30 / 12.15	Military and Educational Training. M.O.s inspection - two Coys on fatigue at Bn. Football Ground - Afternoon. Final of Div Cup.	
	23	09.00 / 12.15	Route March - Afternoon Recreational Training	
	24	08.30 / 12.00	Military and Educational Training. M.O.s Inspection. Afternoon - Recreational Training	

Army Form C. 2118.

WAR DIARY
or
INTELLIGENCE SUMMARY.
(Erase heading not required.)

Instructions regarding War Diaries and Intelligence Summaries are contained in F. S. Regs., Part II. and the Staff Manual respectively. Title pages will be prepared in manuscript.

Place	Date	Hour	Summary of Events and Information	Remarks and references to Appendices
	1918 January			
GRAMMONT	25	08.30 12.00	Military and Educational Training. Afternoon - Educational Training	
	26	09.45	Divine Service in Recreation Hall. Record of Football Matches for Div. Cup - Ronse b. Grevin, Goals for 25, Goals against 6	
	27	08.30 13.00	Military and Educational Training - Afternoon - Recreational Training	
	28		5th Battn had the use of the Baths. Cross Country Run for A&B Coys. Cleaning of Lewis Guns	
	29		Cross Country Run for C&D Coys. Military, Educational and Recreational Training	
	30	09.00	Route march. Afternoon Recreational Training	
	31	08.30 13.15	Military Training. Educational and Recreational Training in Afternoon	

D.D. Silva
Lieut. Colonel
4 Seaforth Highlanders
COMMANDING

WAR DIARY
or
INTELLIGENCE SUMMARY.
(Erase heading not required.)

Army Form C. 2118.

Place	Date	Hour	Summary of Events and Information	Remarks and references to Appendices
GRAMMONT	1919 January		Movement of Officers during the month	
	1		2/Lieut J Seaton (4th Gordons) Evacuated to U.K. 11-12-18	
	8		Lieut Col J.M. Mackenzie D.S.O. (12th Royal Scots) Evacuated to U.K.	
	13		2/Lt P.M. Drummond (3rd R.W.) } to U.K. for Demob.	
			Capt J.D. Burridge (3rd Bn Staffs) }	
	18		Lieut J.W. Arnott (YYY) to U.K. for Demobilisation	
	21		Capt N.C.S. Down (4th Gordons) to U.K. for Demobilisation	
	24		2/Lt John Gourlay (14th R.H.) to U.K. for Demob	
	25		2/Lt St Astomis (4th B.W.) to U.K. for Demob	
	28		2/Lt J.D. Davidson (5th B.W.) to U.K. for Demob	

B Ogilvie Lieut. Colonel.
Comdg. 1/1st (Fife & Forfar Yeo.) Battn.
ROYAL HIGHLANDERS

Army Form C. 2118.

WAR DIARY
or
INTELLIGENCE SUMMARY.
(Erase heading not required.)

Place	Date	Hour	Summary of Events and Information	Remarks and references to Appendices
GRAMMONT	1919 February 1	08.30 13.00	Military and Educational Training. Afternoon Half Holiday	
	2		Divine Service	
	3	08.30 13.00	Military and Educational Training. Afternoon Recreational Training	
	4		Route March.	
	5		Military and Educational Training	
	6		Recreational Training and Inter-Squadron Return on Both Runs }	
	7		of Blankets.	
	8		Route March - Afternoon Half Holiday	
	9		Divine Service	
	10	0900 13.00	Military, Educational and Recreational (Inter-Squadron Cross Country Run.) Training	
	11			
	12			
	13			
	14	0900 13.00	Route March. - Afternoon Recreational Training	
	15		Military, Educational and Recreational	
	16		Divine Service.	

722

D.O.O.Wilvie Lieut: Colonel
Comdg. 14th. (Fife & Forfar Yeo) Battn.
ROYAL HIGHLANDERS

WAR DIARY
or
INTELLIGENCE SUMMARY
(Erase heading not required.)

Army Form C. 2118.

Place	Date	Hour	Summary of Events and Information	Remarks and references to Appendices
GRAMMONT	17			
	18	0900 / 13.00	Military, Educational and Recreational Training. Route march, Afternoon Recreational Training.	
	19		Military, Educational and Recreational Training	
	20		{ Inspection of Rifles and Fire Arms by Officer from R.O.A.P. Remounts. Arrangements Re: Cleaning of Billets and Recreational training.	
	21			
	22			
	23		Military Educational and Recreational Training. Divine Service.	
	24			
	25		} Military, Educational and Recreational Training.	
	26			
	27			
	28		Route march. Afternoon - Recreational training.	

A.O.Gibb. Lieut: Colonel
Commd., 14th (Fife & Forfar Yeo) Battn.
ROYAL HIGHLANDERS

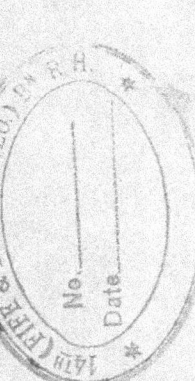

WAR DIARY
or
INTELLIGENCE SUMMARY
(Erase heading not required.)

Army Form C. 2118.

Place	Date	Hour	Summary of Events and Information	Remarks and references to Appendices
GRAMMONT			Movement of Officers during the month.	Mi Bridges
	6.1.19		Lt. Col. R. H. Ross (2nd B.W) Ja.g. 21sg/9338 (O'struck off)	
	7		Lieut. W. Birrell (Fif.Yeo) (3rd Bn.) Seconded to U.K.	
	13		2/Lt. R. Thomson (Fif.Yeo) (3rd Bn.) to U.K. for Demobilisation	
	13		Lieut. E.J. Farquhar (Fif.Yeo) to U.K. for Demobilisation	
	15		2/Lt. W. Reid (Fif.Yeo) do	
	20		2/Lt. W.D. McEwan (Fif.Yeo) (3rd Bn.) Proceeded to U.K. on Conducting duty	
	21-1-19		Capt. J. Ross (4th Gordons) do	
	24-1-19		2/Lt. N.C.O. Souter (11th Bn.) Proceeded to U.K. for Demobilisation	
	25-1-19		2/Lt. G.M. Cowley (4th Bn.) do	
	26-1-19		2/Lt. A. Adamson (7th Bn.) do	
	22-2-19		2/Lt. J. Davidson (3rd Bn.) do	
	26.2.19		2/Lt. E.A. Mellette (3rd Bn.) to U.K. on Conducting duty	
	28.2.19		2/Lt. W.B. Clayton do	
			a/Major Sir W.A.P. Campbell Bt. M.C. To U.K. for Demobilization D.P.O.Blue	

Lieut. Colonel
Comm'd. 14th. (Fife & Forfar Yeo.) Batt'n.
ROYAL HIGHLANDERS

Head Quarters,
29 Brigade

Herewith please War Diary for
month of March 1919.

Wormiston
Capt.
Adjutant (Fife and Forfar Yeo.) 14th R.H.

Army Form C. 2118.

1st/9th Roy Highrs
MARCH 1919

WAR DIARY
INTELLIGENCE SUMMARY.
(Erase heading not required.)

Instructions regarding War Diaries and Intelligence Summaries are contained in F. S. Regs., Part II. and the Staff Manual respectively. Title pages will be prepared in manuscript.

Place	Date 1919 March	Hour	Summary of Events and Information	Remarks and references to Appendices
GRAMMONT	1	0830-1200	Educational & Military Training. Afternoon recreational	
	2		Divine Service	
	3	0900	Batn fatigue	
	4	0830-1200	Military Training - Afternoon recreational training	
	5	0900-1200	Military Training - Inspection of Draft for Army of Occupation. Afternoon recreational training.	
	6	0900-1200	Coy & Platoon Drill - Lecture 1100-1200. Afternoon recreational training.	
	7	0900	Coy & Platoon Drill. Lecture last hour. Afternoon recreational training	
	8	1200	Divine Service	
	9			
	10		Military Training. Draft under Lt. Dané - Lecture. Afternoon recreational training	
	11	0900	Run under Coy Arrangements. Thereafter Cleaning billets & equipment	
	12		Military, Educational, Recreational training. Baths in Afternoon	
	13		Route March & Recreational training	
	14		Military, Educational & Recreational training	
	15		Divine Service	
	16		All available men on coal fatigue	
	17		Run under Coy Arrangements	
	18		Parades under Coy for arrangements. M.O's inspection	
	19		Draft for Army of Occupation, 1 Officer & 95 other ranks left for 8th Batn Black Watch.	
	20		Baths, Cleaning billets &c	
	21		} Batt'y so small all other ranks engaged on regimental duty or fatigues	
	22			
	23			
	24			
	25			
	26			
	27			
	28			
	29			
	30			
	31			

Army Form C. 2118.

WAR DIARY
or
INTELLIGENCE SUMMARY.
(Erase heading not required.)

Instructions regarding War Diaries and Intelligence Summaries are contained in F. S. Regs., Part II. and the Staff Manual respectively. Title pages will be prepared in manuscript.

Place	Date 1919	Hour	Summary of Events and Information	Remarks and references to Appendices
GRAMMONT	March		Movement of Officers during month.	
	3.3.19		Lieut A.S. MacKenzie (15th B.W.) struck off Auth AG/2158/9338(0)	
	4.3.19		2/Lt E.P. Brown (6th B.W.) do 11.2.19	
	5.3.19		2/Lt R. Brown M.C. (4th B.W.) Auth AF21 Disposal Station, Kinross	
	6.3.19		Capt R. Corcoran C.F. proceeded on leave & to Educational Course Oxford.	
	10.3.19		Lieut C.S.R. Oman (10th B.W.) struck off Auth A.G. 2158/9448'960)	
	11.3.19		2/Lt G Anderson proceeded for duty with Chinese Labour Corps.	
			Capt Edwards R.A.M.C. proceeded to Cologne.	
	18.3.19		Lieut R.M. Daniel 3rd B.W. evacuated to U.K.	
	20.3.19		Lieut G.D.M. Beanish (4th B.W.) struck off from 17.3.19.	
	21.3.19		Capt W.T. Lawrence (10 B.W.) proceeded to join 8th Black Watch.	
	23.3.19		2/Lt H. Main (2/13 B.W.) proceeded to U.K. for demobilisation.	
			2/Lt G.S. WALKER (3rd B.W.)	
			2/Lt W.O. FRASER (2nd B.W.)	
			2/Lt S.E. MASSON (4th B.W. (attd)) } Proceeded to join 6th Black Watch	
			2/Lt J.S. MATTHEWSON (2 B.W.)	
			2/Lt P.W. DONE (3 B.W.)	
	24.3.19		Lieut J. Thomson (3/7 B.W.) proceeded to U.K. for demobilisation	
	26.3.19		2/Lieut J. RIDD (2 B.W.) proceeded to join 8th Black Watch	
	31.3.19		2/Lt G.A. McILHATTON (2 B.W.) } proceeded to U.K. for demobilisation	
			Lieut D. McLAREN (6 B.W.)	

Head Quarters
229 Brigade

HZ/62
30/4/19

Herewith please War Diary
for month of April 1919.

J Wormiston
Capt.
Adjt 14th (Fife and Forfar Yeo) Bn R.H

Army Form C. 2118.

14th Q [Regiment?]

WAR DIARY
INTELLIGENCE SUMMARY
(Erase heading not required.)

Instructions regarding War Diaries and Intelligence Summaries are contained in F. S. Regs., Part II. and the Staff Manual respectively. Title pages will be prepared in manuscript.

Place	Date	Hour	Summary of Events and Information	Remarks and references to Appendices
GRAMMONT BELGIUM.	1919 APR 1		All available men on fatigues	
	2		Baths at disposal of Battn.	
	3		Fatigues and regimental duties engaged all men.	
	4			
	5		Church parade	
	6		Fatigues and other employment.	
	7			
	8		Fumigation of blankets at Field Ambulance.	
	9		Usual duties.	
	10			
	11			
	12		Church parade (voluntary)	
	13		1st draft left for demobilization	
	14			
	15		Usual employment of all men not on regimental duties	
	16			
	17			
	18		Good Friday. Whole holiday.	
	19		Routine as usual.	
	20		Church services	
	21		Easter Monday. Whole holiday.	
	22			
	23		Men's routine and duties.	
	24			
	25		Baths allotted to Battn.	
	26		Usual duties	
	27		Church services.	
	28		Usual duties. Battn. so much reduced that all available men not engaged on	
	29			
	30		usual regimental duties were required for fatigues	

[signature] Capt.
aque Colonel
[Commanding] 14th [Bn] [Gordon?] [Highlanders?]
ROYAL HIGHLANDERS

Army Form C. 2118

WAR DIARY
INTELLIGENCE SUMMARY
(Erase heading not required.)

Place	Date	Hour	Summary of Events and Information	Remarks and references to Appendices
GRAMMONT BELGIUM	APRIL 1919		Movement of Officers during month.	
	3.4.19.		Capt. G.J. Rowan, M.C. (2nd B.W.) proceeded to U.K. for demobilization	
	8.4.19.		2/Lieut W.B. Clayton (1st B.W.) } do.	
			2/Lieut W.D. McEwan (7/12 R.Hdrs) }	
	11.4.19		Lieut J.B. Brown M.C. rejoined from Educational centre at Oxford.	
	13.4.19		do. proceeded to join 8 B. The Black Watch	
	23.4.19		Lieut Col. D.D. Ogilvie proceeded on leave to U.K. 23.4.19 – 7.5.19	
	29.4.19		2/Lieut W.O. Gilchrist proceeded to U.K. on leave 15.19 – 15.5.19.	

14 R dpe H/gh Army Form C. 2118.

WAR DIARY
INTELLIGENCE SUMMARY
(Erase heading not required.)

724

Place	Date	Hour	Summary of Events and Information	Remarks and references to Appendices
GRAMMONT BELGIUM	1919 MAY		Battalion is very much reduced and with the exception of several detached men is about to Cadre Establishment. All ranks regimentally employed on various duties, and consequently no parades of any military nature are held. The Births in Grammont are at the disposal of the unit for certain hours each week. As numbers are small church parades are voluntary. Leave to U.K. is open and during the month seven other ranks have proceeded on ordinary leave.	
	May 9		A native bar in own establishment took place and incompliance of other ranks who despatched for demobilization today.	
	24		The civilian open air baths were opened certain hours each day for the benefit of soldiers.	
			Movement of Officers during month	
	May 11		Lieut H/ Travis proceeded to U.K. for repatriation U.K.	
	16		Lt Col A J Ogilvie returned from leave in U.K.	
	18		2/Lieut W.O. Gilchrist Do Do	
	31		2/Lieut J Burnside proceeded to U.K. for repatriation to N.H.	

www.ingramcontent.com/pod-product-compliance
Lightning Source LLC
Chambersburg PA
CBHW081455160426
43193CB00013B/2486